DOPE & DANGEROUS

DOPE & DANGEROUS

No one knows the feeling of borrowed time like those living in
black skin.
We're taught to cherish the mornings like treasures we didn't ask for;
conditioned to carry ourselves with confidence and caution.
We always fear but rarely can we afford to fear out loud.
Since birth, our demise has been on its way and we know it.
The violence that hangs over our heads like fruit from poplar trees,
ignites a relentless desire to make the most of the scraps we have
with America pressing against us, we weave a culture of our own by
dancing to the war drums that play in the background of our lives, by
singing from the parts of our souls that haven't been compromised,
beautiful, ourselves.

In all of the attempts for us to lose ourselves we found something beautiful, ourselves.

BLACK DIAMOND

Hell might be outside your window.

Demons might take the form of family and friends.

You might be in so much pain that it feels like God went on vacation again.

When it feels like you have nowhere to turn or no one that you can trust,

keep in mind that you musn't give up.

You are truly a jewel.

A black diamond currently in the rough.

OGS

OGs are supposed to show you how to grow

OGs aren't supposed to show you how to sell dope

OGs mentor and keep you on the right path

OGs aren't supposed to glorify quick cash

OGs see you shining, and they applaud

OGs don't get jealous when you finally get on

OGs take care of their responsibilities without complaint

OGs don't run from their duties to relive their younger days

OGs will tell you to stay focused and stay in school

If your "OG" doesn't do any of that, they're not an OG, they're just older than you.

K.K.K.K

Kings Killing Kings that's what they see us as.

We want to fight if someone stares too long as we walk past.

Ready to kill if we feel violated or disrespected.

We're willing to take a life to protect a watch or a necklace.

Prepared to do a bid to uphold the code

But what if we flipped the script and turned ops into bros?

Could you imagine the power we'd have as one?

Police would think twice before they pulled their gun.

This country wouldn't know what to do; they would truly be stuck.

Kings Keeping Kings Kings, that ~~could~~ will be us.

A REMINDER THAT'S FRIENDLY

This is just a reminder that the hood was specifically engineered and designed by racist legislators to keep Black and Brown people oppressed, poorly fed, and without quality education.

You're better than that.

SING

You have a song inside of you.

It beats like Metro Boomin;

It flows like when Kendrick is tuned in;

Holy like The Rapper that was given a Chance.

If your soul were a dance, it would be the electric slide.

An irresistible vibe.

That can set off a chain reaction of love.

You can change the world with your song.

Sing.

THE MAN THAT WE ALL KNOW

Brown skin with a mug that only momma could love;

Pains weighing on his face, smile couldn't get up,

His only friend was his gin,

He kept a bottle in his hand

And took a sip for every sin

Ah man, Ah man, he already let the devil in.

ABANDONMENT IN PRIDE

Oh, pride. Oh, pride. Oh, pride.

How did we get here?

I thought the last time was the last time,

That I let you:

Block my blessing

Lock me away from love

Stock up thousands of apologies that I needed to give out

I allowed you to take too much control.

All because I was told: "Be proud like a man should be."

Now I'm old - Here I stand,

A single flower in the desert sand.

Alone.

MORE THAN AN ATHLETE

With all due respect, I may be tall and Black, but I'm not the athlete
you think I am.

My eyes dribble across pages of Richard Wright.

I keep score of my credit and watch stocks as they fall and rise.

In tough situations, I choose to tackle instead of run.

I jump for the stars, and I plan on rebounding one.

Although I may look like the athletes, you see on the screen

I'm not them, and they too are more than they seem.

Scholars, Artists, Businessman and more.

I exist in spaces that are beyond what society set forth.

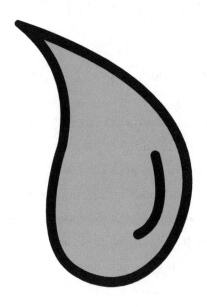

STRENGTH OF LETTING GO

Tears weigh more than a ton.
I'm strong enough to keep them in
but not strong enough to let them run
I have the strength I need to fight back feelings of pain
but I'm still working towards allowing my eyes to rain.
A captive to my own strength, is that what I've become?
Is that really being strong? Or does power come from allowing
yourself to feel?
Maybe strength comes from letting go and not holding on.

DON'T WAIT FOR HER

Don't wait for America.

She doesn't see you how momma sees you.

She doesn't know love how love is known to be.

She's been running for so long that now her greatest fear
is stopping.

Stopping would mean seeing you.

Facing what she's done to you.

She would see the absence of every promise she ever made.

She would have to redefine herself in a way that included you.

Don't wait for America. She never waited for you.

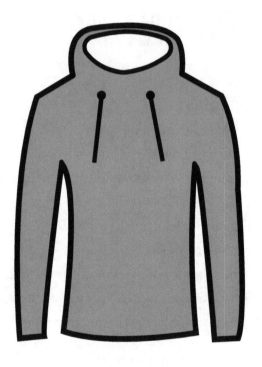

FASHIONABLY BLACK

The clothes that decorate my black body carry a piece of
my soul.
Shirts rest over shoulders that supported inexplicable weights.
Pants hugging legs that have stood the trials of a life that
exceeded American limits.
Sneakers protecting feet that have traveled miles of danger
and violence.
Clothes that decorate my living Black body must celebrate
my survival.
Clothes that decorate my living black body carry a piece of
my soul.
A soul that must be celebrated.

PARENTS DON'T ALWAYS UNDERSTAND

Can't blame mother or father

They only knew a practical life

A life structured around lights, gas, and rent

Around interview, hire, fire, salary, and retirement

I have dreams bigger than they were taught to understand.

I fear to tell them that my destiny isn't grounded in tradition.

It sits within the castle that was cast in the sky by their sacrifice.

They afforded me bigger dreams than they can understand,

and now what's necessary for me to be successful requires their

disappointment.

VOLCANO OF TRUTH

There's a pending explosion in every spirit that holds in their truth.

Truth stacks high and expands wide and cannot be detained for long
without it destroying some part of its host;

Without it becoming contaminated with anger.

Truth, when delivered on time renders freedom that can echo
throughout your days.

The time for truth is always now because your freedom is always
at stake.

FEAR OF GOD

Black is love

Black is us

They pack the cells

They trapping us

They shoot us down

They blast the gun

You see my hands

What more you want?

I know it's fear it's coming from

You pull me over, my heart it

pumps

Not sure if I was meant to die

— Jokes on you I'm still alive!

And I'm black

I'm blessed

Despite the weather

I stand

In joy

I smile whenever

They thought

They had

Me down

But never

Do we submit

Or do we

Give up

I stand
I fight
I look in the mirror
I see the God
That you're in fear of.
I stand
I fight
I look in the mirror
I see the God
That you're in fear of.

I REMAIN

We cry
We sweat
We bled for this
We left the shackles
We kept the whips
We kept the chains
We kept the chains
Check the last
We kept the names
See my eyes
We kept the flame
Deep inside
We kept the pain

Since X was shot
Since Pac was slain
But that's alright
Because I remain.

REALITY'S UNFORTUNES

When you're born in poverty
It's like the lottery to get out
Trapping in the trap
Getting it in is how you get out
Sometimes you'll feel like the baby
That Brenda had spit out
When the system is built against you
You gotta figure this shit out
B'fore the bullets catch up
Or the law get you
You'll spend nights talking to the ceiling
Praying that the Lord hears you
You're going to need some guidance

Surrounded by this violence

And all types of trauma

Looking to find ways to deal

But how could you start to heal, when you weren't taught to feel?

THE WANTS

I want mad money.

I want all my friends who rap to get discovered.

I want dealers to stop pushing dope.

I want pastors to stop pushing hope.

I want my people who've been traumatized to cope.

I want to de-stigmatize being broke,

And to stop using the term "woke."

I want to stop glorifying being rich and be okay with ownership and
being out of debt.

I want to be my definition of cool.

I want my kids to not have to pay for school.

I want all of these things and add more to the list.

Everyday I try to make a decision that'll make the world more like this.

THE ONE-SIDED CONVERSATION

"You should smile"

"Why you look so angry?"

"You're too beautiful to be out here by yourself."

"Damn, you look sexy Miss."

"Excuse me, can I talk to you for a second?"

Kissing sounds

Whistles

She walks away. But before she escapes from earshot of him, he tells her what he thinks of himself.

"Bitch!"

CONCRETE JUNGLE

Dad said, "Steel birds patrol the sky."

Their eyes are bright and wide

They fly at night and their wings are loud

When they're in the sky sirens are on the ground

My brother said, "Watch out for the snakes because they bite."

I heard a woman say, "All niggas are dogs; don't think twice."

Mother: "Don't be like the monkeys hanging on the corner."

The "monkeys": "School is where the sheep go to wander"

Uncle: "You have the heart of a lion" and I wasn't sure what

that meant

Was I the king of a jungle that I didn't know I was living in?

Was my life in danger? Why did I need so much advice?

Someone ran by and yelled "You pigs won't take my life!"

I looked at my hands. To the mirror I ran.

I checked to see if I was one of the animals that everyone could not seem to stand.

I seen no signs of a beast whatsoever.

Am I going crazy? Did my sanity fumble?

Or am I living in what they call the concrete jungle?

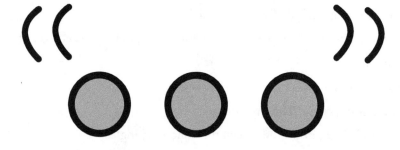

ALL WE NEED TO DO IS

Never trust a person who starts a sentence with the phrase…

"All we need to do is…"

Especially when they're talking about revolution.

BLACK SYNOPSIS

Your kinks are crowns.

The color of love is brown.

The harmony that sings in your heart may it never come down.

The hood is a kingdom that others will overtake if they could.

Prisons are mansions shared by the misunderstood.

Gangs are the same as political parties,

they just war on blocks instead of entire countries.

Our art is a language not a commodity for capitalists.

If you sell yourself short, people will take advantage of it.

You are an embodiment of freedom fought for over the years.

You are the result of your ancestors' Blood Sweat & Tears.

CHANGE IN DIET

We're ordering music off of the dollar menu

Watching shows that have no nutritional value

We digest pictures and captions that will never leave us full

We want everything microwaved because waiting for quality is old

People are dying younger and younger, we see it every evening

I look around, and I think to myself "Maybe I should go vegan."

PASSPORT

Someone told me: Baldwin went to Paris to write.

To which I replied: But I don't have a passport.

Someone said: Then what are all those books?

Find a corner and take flight in chapters to Paris and beyond.

IT AIN'T ABOUT

It ain't about guns

It ain't about the weight

It ain't about who's a G

It ain't about who caught a case

It ain't about who shot who

Or who spent time in the cage

They rather see us beef

Then standing on stage

A gun pops

A body drops

Another in the grave

Poor killing poor

That's how they set the game.

HEAVENLY CONVERSATIONS

Where Jesus at?

Does he look like what the reverend tells the congregation?

Does he really care about tithes in comparison to the money
people are making?

Oh snap, is that Dr. King?... I wonder if he has any regrets about
integration.

If I were alive at that time, I definitely would've voted bro.

I know Malcolm is looking from the side of eyes saying "I told
you so."

Damn! Only if the upper room had visiting hours.

Every time I was confused, I'd just come through and get to
the knowledge.

I guess that's the point of being down here.

Take it one day at a time until your time is near.

GOD INSIDE

I've been looking for God. I heard he's been looking for me
I can't seem to find him. Where am I supposed to be?
I pray and I prayed. I got down on my knees
Turns out all along he was inside of me.
Mirror mirror on the wall
I didn't know you were God all along
This world told me to be humble
To try to suffocate you
They told me to "chill" whenever I tried to embrace you
They told me that you were in the church
They said that I should read the Bible
They told me that you were in the sky
I think they tried to hide you

If I knew that I was you and you were I
I could've started to put together the question, "Who am I?"
Undiscovered galaxies right inside my mind.
The glory of the Nile river flows down my spine.
Skin tinted from the eternal sun.
Now I look in the mirror and I see the one.

WHAT'S FREE?

What's Free?

I'm asking for a friend.

They got him locked down.

He can't even use a pen.

If he would've gone to trial,

I'd probably never see him again.

Justice ain't blind.

They saw the color of his skin.

THE VOID WITHIN

Everybody wants a big-body Bentley

And a house to park it in

We tend to get lost in grandiose thoughts of when

we acquire every desire that's on our heart and then

We realize that shit doesn't even start to fill the real void that's within.

Material things are like Black Lives to the American government.

They don't really matter.

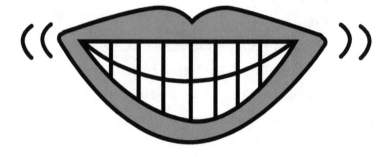

I SMILE

The thickness of the armor that coats my flesh

is also the distance at which I must keep the world.

Although I don't know why they continue to form weapons against

me, I know too well that they plan for my black demise.

Still, I smile. Still, I rise.

Their efforts are futile. Their justifications are as fragile as their egos.

Their world shatters at the thought of them waking up and realizing,

they're not as special as the image they created for themselves.

All the while I smile. Bright. Bold. Black. I smile.

THANK YOU.

CPSIA information can be obtained
at www.ICGtesting.com
Printed in the USA
LVHW062240220419
615090LV00005B/234/P

9 781798 145630